LETTER TO THE LORD ADVOCATE,

REGARDING THE

SCHOOLS ON THE SCHEME OF THE SOCIETY IN SCOTLAND FOR PROPAGATING CHRISTIAN KNOWLEDGE.

Directors of the Society.

EDINBURGH, 49 QUEEN STREET,
19th December 1867.

To

THE RIGHT HON. THE
LORD ADVOCATE FOR SCOTLAND.

MY LORD,

The Directors of the "Society in Scotland for Propagating Christian Knowledge" have had their attention called to the terms in which the Society and its operations have been spoken of in the Reports issued by Her Majesty's Commissioners appointed to inquire into the Schools in Scotland, and more particularly to those passages which will be found at pages 35, 75, and 168, of their Second Report, and which are as follows :—

(1.) "The Christian Knowledge Society is a Society which was instituted in 1709 for the purpose of promoting religious knowledge in the Highlands and Islands, and is by law connected with the Established Church. The Society, however, has a permanent income, and is not dependent merely on private contribution. The Society does not take much advantage of the Privy Council grants. On these Schools the Assistant Commissioners observe, ' It is impossible to form a correct estimate of the teaching in the Society's Schools, as we were able only to report on seven in all ; and though the teaching of four of these schools is considered good, and only one is considered bad, yet the impression left upon the mind is that, as schools, they are not quite so efficient as the General Assembly schools or the Free Church schools, though the average income is very much the same as in the General Assembly schools.' "

(2.) "The oldest of these Societies in the Highlands is the Society for Propagating Christian Knowledge. This Society was instituted in the year 1709, for the express purpose of supplying the means of education and of religion in the Highlands and Islands, and other remote corners of Scotland, and of teaching girls the industrial branches of education.

"The Society has now an income of nearly £7000 per annum, £3481 of which, in 1865, was applied in aid of 249 individuals, who are the teachers of the Society ; the men receiving rather under £20 per annum each on an average, and the women under £8. Although the improvement of the islanders was a special object with the founders of this Society, the sum expended in the Hebrides in 1865 was only £445, including £103 of superannuation allowances. The number of its schools indeed is very limited. Mr Nicolson in this district found only 17, and their condition on the whole was very unsatisfactory. Mr Menzies, the Inspector appointed by the Society to examine their schools, in his examination before us, expressed the same opinion. He said that 'the education in the Society's schools in the Hebrides is of a very low character indeed,' and that 'it is the exception to the rule that we have had what can be called an efficient teacher in these districts.' Such testimony, coming from persons who cannot be charged with any unfriendly bias, excites a feeling of regret that a Society endowed with funds so considerable, and instituted for the express purpose of diffusing education in these destitute districts, should have fallen so short of the design of its original founders.

"It is erroneous to assume that the low educational condition of the Highland population can justify the employment of teachers who have little learning, who are devoid of energy, and who are without aptitude or training in the art of communicating instruction. When such persons are selected for schools in the Islands, there is little wonder that they become merely the recipients of the annual allowance from the Society, and not agents for promoting the education of the young.

"When the unusual difficulties that a teacher has to encounter in the Highlands are taken into account, it is evident that though it may not be necessary to seek for men of high acquirements, an endeavour should be made to obtain persons who have not only been thoroughly grounded in the elementary branches of education, and the art of teaching, but are distinguished by energy and ability to impart the knowledge which they have themselves acquired."

(3.) "It will be observed also that the sum contributed by the Society for Propagating Christian Knowledge is set down at £342, which is the amount at present obtained from this source. As we have already pointed out, this Society was founded for the express purpose of promoting education in these destitute districts, and it must be admitted that £342 (or £445, including retiring pensions,) is but an insignificant proportion of a total income of £7000 a year. There seems no reason to doubt that a much larger sum might be spared from the funds of this Society to meet the urgent claim of these Islands ; in the meantime, however, we prefer to estimate the aid from this Society at the amount actually received."

These passages show the Commissioners to be so little acquainted with the history and objects of the Society, and the state of the Society's Schools, that the Directors deem it right to make the following statement, in order to remove the erroneous and unjust impression which the passages above quoted are calculated to convey.

I. Through the passages above quoted there seems to run the assumption that the Society may expend the whole or whatever portion of its funds it pleases upon any one particular district of the country marked off for this purpose. But the case is far otherwise ; for,

(1.) The Royal Patents in favour of the Society bear that its field of operation is to be the *whole of Scotland*, special regard being had to the Highlands, Islands, and those remote corners " where error, idolatry, superstition, and ignorance do most abound, by reason of the largeness of parishes and scarcity of schools."

(2.) A large proportion of the Society's income arises from legacies, mortifications, and bequests, *the terms of which fix the objects and particular localities upon which the money thus derived must be expended.* The Society is merely the administrator of those funds, and has no power to allocate them otherwise. This is the reason why a very few of the Schools are situated in districts which may not seem to stand much in need of aid.

(3.) Schools are not the only agency employed to carry out the purposes for which the Society was founded. Her Majesty's Commissioners, in referring to the expenditure of the Society's income, appear to lose sight of this fact. Had they looked at the Scheme of the Society, they would have seen that a large sum is devoted—*in terms of the deeds by which it is derived*—to the maintenance of Ministers, Missionaries, and Catechists, and also to Foreign Missions and Schools.

II. It has been made matter of blame by the Commissioners that the Society should have had so few Schools in the Hebrides.

It is allowed that the Society's Schools in these islands—though more numerous than the Commissioners have reckoned them to be—are yet fewer than they were previous to the Secession from the Church in 1843. That event deprived the Society of most of their teachers, as well as in many instances of the school buildings. The Schools continued to be taught as before, but thenceforth in connexion with the Free Church. From that date to the present, the Directors of the Society have been so far from being indifferent to the educational wants of those islands, that in no single instance of application for aid from their funds have they refused it, provided only even moderately sufficient school accommodations were offered. The supply of such accommodations the Society has no power to enforce, and the want of these must, of course, prove a serious obstacle to efficient teaching.

Whatever educational destitution, therefore, may exist in the Hebrides—and happily it is not nearly so great as was anticipated—is not to be attributed in any respect as matter of blame to the Society.

III. As to the statements made by the Commissioners with regard to the general efficiency of the Society's Schools, the Society's Directors would observe :—

(1.) That in the first of the passages quoted from the Commissioners' Report, it is stated that "only seven in all were reported on," and yet it is added, "though the teaching of four of these Schools is considered good, and only one is considered bad, yet the impression left upon mind is, that, as schools, they are not quite so efficient as the General Assembly schools or the Free Church schools."

When it is remembered that out of upwards of 250 Society Schools only *seven* are here reported on, and that of these seven only *one* can be considered *bad*, it does afford matter of surprise to the Directors that such a conclusion should have been reached from such premises, or a comparison like this made upon information so slender.

(2.) In the second passage quoted above, the following statement occurs: " Mr Nicolson in this district (*i.e.* in the Hebrides) found only seventeen, and their condition on the whole was very unsatisfactory." On referring to Mr Nicolson's Report, we find that he expresses himself in terms considerably different, and thus : " The condition and efficiency of these schools cannot on the whole be considered satisfactory." And this opinion seems to be based very much, if not almost entirely, on the evidence given by Mr Menzies, the Society's former Inspector ; for, in the detailed portion of Mr Nicolson's Report, we can find little to justify even this modified statement, and certainly nothing to account for the terms in which these Schools are spoken of by the Commissioners themselves.

The passages quoted from Mr Menzies' evidence, (which, it must be remembered, refers to the Schools in the Hebrides alone,) *taken, as they are, by themselves and apart from the other statements made by him at the same time* to the Commissioners, may tend to convey an unfavourable impression of the schools in these Islands. But it is proper to observe, that, in a communication addressed by Mr Menzies to the Directors, he explains his evidence thus :—

"I think that I have just cause of complaint that the Commissioners should have selected two isolated sentences from the evidence which they required me to give before them, for the purpose of making remarks damaging to the Society generally. If the context of the evidence which they quote for this purpose is perused, it will show that while I frankly admitted that the Society's schools were not in a satisfactory condition, I at the same time stated that the result of this information having been obtained by the Directors, was, the removal of unsatisfactory teachers, and the appointment of others in their place. The remarks made in the Commissioners' Report as to the qualifications of teachers are truisms with which the Directors have long been familiar; and in the evidence which I gave before the Commissioners, I pointed out the great difficulties under which the Society laboured, and the obstacles which lay in the way of getting men of such qualifications as the Commissioners recommend."

"In judging of statements such as the evidence laid before the Commissioners, it must be kept in mind that these statements are, after all, only matters of opinion, differing in each case according to the standard of excellence which each witness sets before him; and as I had, before filling the office of your Inspector, visited with my late father the parochial schools of Aberdeen, Banff, and Morayshires, I had before me a very high standard of excellence. It may be that if I had never visited any but the Long Island schools, I would have expressed myself very differently. But in giving evidence before a Board who were to point out remedial measures, I conceived it to be my duty, considering the immense importance, in a social point of view, of introducing a good system of education into the Hebrides, to set before me such a standard as would, if attained, be the means of producing these social benefits."

The Directors are fully aware that some of the Society's schools in the Hebrides are not equal in efficiency to those in more favoured localities; but the explanation of this is not far to seek, and has been well put by Mr Nicolson in his Report, when he says, "The isolation of their homes, the usually small salary, the inferior accommodation, and the non-payment of school fees, explain the difficulty of procuring for such parishes the services of energetic men of good attainments."

No doubt these difficulties have to be met in the case of the other classes of schools in these localities, and that they are, in general, surmounted by others with no greater success than by the Society, the Directors are assured by information derived from other sources, and also by the evidence afforded in the Reports issued by H. M. Commissioners. The Directors are at a loss, therefore, to comprehend why the schools of the Society should have been so hardly dealt with, and why the Commissioners should have been at such pains to express "a feeling of regret that the Society should have fallen so short of the design of its original founders." A striking commentary on the opinion thus put forth by the Commissioners is afforded by that given by their Assistant Commissioner, who, when speaking of the manner in which the Society has carried out the objects for which it was founded, says, " It has, in pursuance of this object, accomplished a large amount of good, and is entitled to very grateful notice in any account of education in the Highlands."

IV. In judging of the present condition of the Society's schools, it ought not to be forgotten that the object originally aimed at by the Society was to diffuse, as widely as possible, the mere elements of a Christian education. When educational agencies became multiplied in the districts occupied by the Society, and when, from the state of the times, a more extended course of instruction required to be imparted, the Directors of the Society—before a Commission to inquire into the schools in Scotland was spoken of—forthwith gave their attention to raising the character of their schools, and to securing the services of a higher class of teachers. With this end in view, they have held out to men of higher qualifications the inducement of increased salaries, and have added the stimulus of regular and systematic inspection, their schools being now visited by the Society's Inspector as nearly as possible annually.

As a further incitement to diligence, a large sum, in addition to the salaries entered in the Society's Scheme, is set apart annually to be distributed among the teachers, according to the relative state of efficiency of their schools, as ascertained by the Society's Inspector.

The change in the character of their schools, which they are thus gradually effecting, is not one which could be accomplished in a day. They could not throw at once upon the world a large and deserving class of men, who, though as suitable teachers as could be procured at the time of their appointment, were not perhaps in some cases possessed of sufficient attainments to meet the requirements of the present day ; but, whenever the Directors have seen their way to superannuate these, or when vacancies have occurred through death or otherwise, in making new appointments, they have used every means to procure the services of men of higher qualifications. The Directors have found it a matter of the utmost difficulty to obtain such men for the more remote localities, and nothing has tended to retard their efforts more than a want of adequate accommodations,—the supply of which, as before stated, they have no means of enforcing.

Further, the Directors deem it due to themselves to assert, and they do so, without fear of contradiction, that, within recent years, no schools in the country have made correspondingly greater progress than those under their management.

V. Before concluding these observations, the Directors would call attention to the manner in which the Society schools are entered in the Table appended to the Second Report of H. M. Commissioners. These schools, instead of being classified under the head of "Church of Scotland Schools," have been classified under the head of "Undenominational and others;" in disregard of the source of the funds with which they are maintained, and of the legally established connexion of this Society with the Church of Scotland.

I have the honour to be,

MY LORD,

Your Lordship's most obedient Servant,

In name and by appointment of the Directors,

JAS. SIMSON, *Chairman.*